SONGBIRDS

A BOOK OF 21 POS[TCARDS]

Salmo trutti

SAN FRANCISCO • CALIFORNIA

Salmo trutti

P.O. BOX 280070
SAN FRANCISCO • CALIFORNIA 94128-0070

ISBN: 1-56313-876-X
TITLE #: ST876

Salmo trutti publishes a large line of photographic books and postcard books.
Please write for more information.

Printed in Korea

SONGBIRDS
Male Common Grackle

PUBLISHED BY *Salmo trutti* • SAN FRANCISCO, CALIFORNIA

SONGBIRDS
Female Goldfinch feeding on thistle seeds

PUBLISHED BY *Salmo trutti* • SAN FRANCISCO, CALIFORNIA

SONGBIRDS
Bohemian Waxwing eating berries

PUBLISHED BY *Salmo trutti* • SAN FRANCISCO, CALIFORNIA

SONGBIRDS
Yellow-shafted Flicker during fall migration

PUBLISHED BY *Salmo trutti* • SAN FRANCISCO, CALIFORNIA

SONGBIRDS
Great Crested Flycatcher, common in open woods

PUBLISHED BY *Salmo trutti* • SAN FRANCISCO, CALIFORNIA

SONGBIRDS
Purple Martin

PUBLISHED BY *Salmo trutti* • SAN FRANCISCO, CALIFORNIA

SONGBIRDS
Yellow-rumped Warbler in winter plumage

PUBLISHED BY *Salmo trutti* • SAN FRANCISCO, CALIFORNIA

SONGBIRDS
Blue Jay on stump

PUBLISHED BY *Salmo trutti* • SAN FRANCISCO, CALIFORNIA

SONGBIRDS
Black-throated Green Warbler in pine tree

PUBLISHED BY *Salmo trutti* • SAN FRANCISCO, CALIFORNIA

SONGBIRDS
Male Evening Grosbeak

PUBLISHED BY *Salmo trutti* • SAN FRANCISCO, CALIFORNIA

SONGBIRDS
Male Robin and young

PUBLISHED BY *Salmo trutti* • SAN FRANCISCO, CALIFORNIA

SONGBIRDS
Red-winged Blackbird

PUBLISHED BY *Salmo trutti* • SAN FRANCISCO, CALIFORNIA

SONGBIRDS
Common Yellow-throated Warbler in beach plum bush

PUBLISHED BY *Salmo trutti* • SAN FRANCISCO, CALIFORNIA

SONGBIRDS
Male Blackpoll Warbler during migration

PUBLISHED BY *Salmo trutti* • SAN FRANCISCO, CALIFORNIA

SONGBIRDS
Cedar Waxwing in rose-hip bush

PUBLISHED BY *Salmo trutti* • SAN FRANCISCO, CALIFORNIA

SONGBIRDS
Yellow-bellied Flycatcher and sumac berry cluster

PUBLISHED BY *Salmo trutti* • SAN FRANCISCO, CALIFORNIA

SONGBIRDS
Male Purple Finch

PUBLISHED BY *Salmo trutti* • SAN FRANCISCO, CALIFORNIA

SONGBIRDS
Female House Finch on bittersweet berry vine

PUBLISHED BY *Salmo trutti* • SAN FRANCISCO, CALIFORNIA

SONGBIRDS
Northern Oriole at nest

PUBLISHED BY *Salmo trutti* • SAN FRANCISCO, CALIFORNIA

SONGBIRDS
Male Cardinal on branch

PUBLISHED BY *Salmo trutti* • SAN FRANCISCO, CALIFORNIA

USA
20
1995

SONGBIRDS
Pair of Tree Swallows on fence

PUBLISHED BY *Salmo trutti* • SAN FRANCISCO, CALIFORNIA